BREAKTHROUGH TO NEW BEGINNINGS

Breakthrough to New Beginnings

A Poet's Journey

JUDITH ANNIQUE FRANÇOIS

Judith Annique François LLC

Copyright © 2021 by Judith Annique François

All rights reserved. No part of this book may be reproduced in any manner whatsoever without written permission except in the case of brief quotations embodied in critical articles and reviews.

Editors: Carla M. Dean,
          Destiny Henry

Published in the United States of America by Judith Annique François LLC

ISBN 978-1-7374616-1-6 (Paperback)
      978-1-7374616-0-9 (Digital)

First Printing, 2021

Contents

A Poet's Journey   1

The Ocean   3
Father   5
Onion Rings   7
Funerals   8
Holding On   11
Rest, My Love   13
Worthy   15
Why Didn't You Talk to Me, Mom?   17
Karma   21
Nothing   23
A Different Kind of Love   25
Used to Be   26
My Beauty Is Not Skin Deep   27
Therapy   28
Safe: A Letter to My Fear   30
So This Is Love   31
Resilience   33
Resistance   34
Community   35
Protest   36
One Life Taken   37
Healing   38
Quiet   39
New Beginnings   41

Later	43
Lifetime	44
Breakthrough	46
Holy Motherfuckers	48
Quiet 2	50
Everything Is Going to Be Okay	51
A Good Cry	52
Dream	53
Breathe	54
Let Go	55
I Hate Writing	56
I Did It Anyway	58
What If It's True	59
Honey	61
Killed by Kindness	62
About The Author	63

A Poet's Journey

I never considered myself a poet, even though I've been writing poems ever since I was a teenager. My poetry is something I've been secretive about, to the point where I never showed anyone because I had already decided my poems were bad. Unfortunately, my insecurity kept me from growing as a poet and deterred me from learning all the different styles and techniques to explore different styles in using my voice to speak on everything I've been holding inside, too afraid to speak of it.

Just a little over two years ago, I *finally* developed a love of reading poetry. I mostly read famous poets, my favorites being Maya Angelou and Langston Hughes. Still, I rarely wrote poetry as I began to pursue my lifelong ambition of writing narratives by journaling accounts of my childhood memories, my healing journey from trauma, and writing about my place of birth, Haiti. At the beginning of studying Creative Writing at Roosevelt University, I never considered taking a poetry class. The horrible events of 2020 changed my mind. Wanting to lighten my workload, I thought poetry could be an outlet to vent about all the things happening around me. It was a stressful year dealing with the global COVID pandemic, a family member's death, and graduate school pressures. I realized that the fall semester would be my last one in graduate school, and if I did not at least *try* poetry, there was a possibility I would never learn what it takes to become a poet. So, I took the leap and signed up.

What I enjoyed most about my poetry workshop class was learning that I *am* a poet, and there is no valid reason to say I am not. I learned that it's okay to break the rules about how and why we use words to express ourselves. Poetry is all about what you make of it. I appreciated the diversity of the types of poetry I got the opportunity to read. They all inspired me not to be afraid of the storyteller that I am.

The Ocean

The ocean is the holder of things
It holds
New things
Old things
Shiny things
Cheap things
Valuable things
Things cherished by some
And abhorred by others

The good thing about the ocean
Is that it does not say no
It welcomes everything
It belongs to everything

It welcomes unwanted things
Forgotten things
Beautiful things
Lost things
Fragile things

The ocean gives and holds life
The ocean also takes life
The ocean is God

The ocean reminds me that
I am all of the things that it holds

The ocean is full of lost souls
It keeps them safe
Like the shiny treasures that it keeps from dying

Sometimes the ocean is blue
It holds all of the world's peace and silence

Sometimes the ocean is green
Because there is a storm brewing inside of it
Even the ocean gets angry
Seeking revenge on all the fools who abuse and take it for granted

At times, the ocean is clear because it feels empty
Even with all the secrets buried deep inside of it

The ocean is mostly water
I am mostly water
I hold secrets deep inside me

If you ever feel the rage inside you
Eating you alive
And the weight of the world is too much to bear
On your tiny shoulders
Do not worry
You can *always* bring them to the ocean

Father

I used to think I did not need a father
But what do I know
I'm just a little girl
Who still cries
Every time she watches
The Color Purple

You know
That scene
Where that lady
Walked inside that church
Singing *that* song

And then
She hugged her father
And said, *"See, Daddy, sinners have soul, too."*

That reminds me
Of how I'm so much more
Then what I've been *made* to believe

I may never get everything I want
And that's fair
Who told me
That I deserve anything
In *this* life?

Who told me that I deserve to be happy?
Who told me that I should be asking anything
From a man whose father died when he was an infant
And whose mother *never* found a replacement?

Who told me that I could blame another
Human being for *my* unhappiness?

I used to think I did not need a father
But what do *I* know

I'm just a little girl who still cries
When she writes silly little poems
About a man who may
Or may not ever
Open *his* heart to her

Onion Rings

Onion Rings have been on my mind lately
My mother liked Onion Rings
She bought them and ate them while they were hot
She bought a bag once
She cooked them and made me try one
I took one small bite and forced it down my throat
I did not eat the rest of my Onion Ring

"It's so good. They're delicious," she said
She tried to convince me
But nothing could make me think that
Onion Rings were anything but gross

Onion Rings have been on my mind lately
So, I bought a bag
I heated my cheap canola oil
I poured a handful of Onion Rings into the hot pan
I scooped the light-brown rings
With a large metal spoon that had holes in it
I rested them on a plate with paper towels to absorb the grease
Hoping I could spare a few calories
Just like my mother used to do

I tried one
Then I ate another
Then I ate some more
I ate the whole bag
It turned out that
Onion Rings are not so bad
Maybe my mom *was* right

Funerals

When I learn I have to go to another funeral
I shake and shiver
I begin to think of all the ways I can avoid going
I think about whether the dead person was important enough
For me to attend their funeral

If I can't avoid it
I go and then I say
This is the last funeral I will go to

On my way to the funeral
I get nervous and overwhelmed with anticipation
I picture what it will be like
I ask myself will this person's
Spirit be there to watch the whole thing
Will they look to see who came to their funeral
And who did not?
Will they even notice me there or care that I came?

As I enter the building
My heart beats fast
When I see the casket
My legs want to turn back and run away

If the casket is open
I try not to look
But my curiosity is
Always too strong

As I walk down the aisle
I feel sick to my stomach
Like there are butterflies in there, but not for the right reason
I feel my throat doing that weird thing
When it feels like someone is choking you but from the inside

I want to go to the bathroom
But I can't
I have to fight to hold my insides in
Long enough to make it to a toilet

As I get closer
I realize it's really real
I no longer have a reason not
To believe they are dead

When I stand in front of them
I look at their face
I am shocked because they don't look like
What I expected them to look like
Most of the time, they don't even look like
They looked when they were alive

I can't help but feel sorry for them
I think about how they were when they were alive
Some of them were strong, vibrant, beautiful
Arrogant, proud, and full of plans
And then I think how sad that
They will never see another tomorrow
I wonder how many times they said
"I'll do it tomorrow."

My heart beats even faster the longer I look at them
Because I know someday
It will be me in a casket
Or coffin
Or whatever you want to call it
I hope I get a beautiful funeral
When I die at 104, of course

Every time I go to a funeral
I think about who will be next
I think about how young I am
And if I live a long life
How many more funerals will I have to attend

I went to a funeral once
Afterward
Strangers bombarded me with kisses and hugs
They told me to be strong,
You are so brave; you're so courageous

A few days after the funeral
Some will call and ask me if I am okay
I tell them yes
But I'm not

After I buried my mother, my stepfather
and a few of my friends
I said to myself
I will never go to another funeral again
But that's a lie
There are too many people
Whom it will kill
If I don't *make* it to *their* funerals

Holding On

A few weeks ago
I wrote you a poem
I guess this is the rest of it
You were here
I was here

Though separated by thousands of miles
Our spirits stayed intertwined
Like a leaf clings on to its branch
From winds and hail
Your roots were strong enough
To hold me tight

Our love was like a river
We flowed through
Different motions
And waves
Tidals made us go separate ways
But we had the same destination
So, I never worried about the waves
Until you went home
Now, most days
I feel like I'm all alone
Must I do this all on my own

I wasn't ready
It wasn't your time
And I know you
Had bigger plans for your life
But maybe God knew something
That we didn't

So, until we meet again
I am holding on
To you
My love

Rest, My Love

Can you see now?
Can you see how much you are loved?
Can you see us?
Can you see *inside* the hearts of your two children?
How much do we miss you?

Do you watch us when we sleep?
Do you *kiss* my forehead and tell me good night?
Is it you that breathe into me
That strength that makes me keep going,
Even when I want to give up?

When I was inside the hurricane
I was scared
I thought the end of my time here was near
But then, I felt something
I smelled sweet flowers and blood
And I knew that it was you
I felt *peace*, and then I went to sleep
Were you behind it all?

When you were here
You were constantly concerned about me
You were terrified
I would have to experience the same things
You went through

I assure you
I am okay
Your time to worry about me is over

You did your job
I got it from here

So, until we meet again
Rest in peace, my love

Worthy

Do you know what your passion is?
Or are you still searching?
Do you water your gifts?
So they can grow
Bringing all of your possibilities
To fruition?

Or do you hide them
Deep inside
Because
You've seen how cruel
This world can be?

If so, I'm here to tell you to STOP!
I mean, GO!
RUN after your dreams

You'll be surprised by
All the treasures you discover
Flabbergasted by all
The people you inspire
And even those who mocked you
Will soon want to join you

So, find your passions
Nourish your gifts
And bless us all with
Your knowledge
Because no matter what
Happens
In the end

You'll see that it was all
Worth it

Why Didn't You Talk to Me, Mom?

My first memory is of you
Running to see me
I stood looking at you
Patiently waiting for you
I wanted to run to you, too
But *Grann* didn't want me to run
Through the slippery, rocky streets
I was almost two years old
Then you fell
Hard on the ground
You hit a big rock
I saw blood coming out of your knees
Running down both of your legs
I don't remember it all, but I think you cried
So, my first memory of you is
Of you getting hurt
And *watching* you get hurt
And I couldn't do anything about it

The next time I remember seeing you was at the airport
You finally came back to Haiti
And when you saw me for the first time
You stopped
You looked like you had seen a ghost
I stood there frozen, too, taking you in
For a second, I thought you were an angel
Then tears poured from your eyes
And finally,
You ran to me

You opened both of your arms and held me tightly
I was nine years old

You smelled so good
And I loved your dark black, silky hair
I felt warm and safe in your arms

The next time I saw you, you cried when he put his hands on you
He touched you
Not the way a lover is supposed to touch his wife
It was all my fault
You asked me to clean the house and make the bed
Before you came home that day
But there were dishes in the sink and the bed wasn't made
My attempt at sweeping the floor was a weak one
When you came home from work,
You were too tired to do the cleaning yourself
Then, he came home
And made you cry

You cried again after I left home
On our first phone call after the day I left
All you could bring yourself to say was, *"Judith"*
And then we both began to cry

I know you cried for me many, many times
I heard you cry one last time after you left us
But I don't know if it was all in my head or
If it was really you

I think of the times when we had the chance
How we wasted it on so many things that didn't matter
Like when you told me that you were like me once
Shy and quiet
I wonder if the same thing that happened to me,
That made me this way
Happened to you

I wished you had talked to me, Mom
You could've told me how you changed
How you went from being silent and afraid to talk like me
To smile even when your heart had so many unhealed wounds

Why didn't you talk to me, Mom?
You didn't have to keep everything a secret
I would've helped you carry them
I would have understood
And maybe you would've learned to understand me, too

Why didn't we have those conversations?
Woman to woman
Mother to daughter
Generation to generation
Friend to friend

We could have been each other's strength
Now my biggest fear is repeating the same mistakes you made
That's why I want to be a mother someday
But then I don't
I don't want to pass this generational curse to another Black woman
Who will not know how to handle it

You were hurt
And I watched you
I couldn't do anything about it

I don't believe in all this religion stuff anymore, Mom
I know it hurts you to hear that
But God has never answered any of my prayers
He abandoned you when you needed Him the most
You prayed so much
You danced and sang for Him
You fasted for Him
You stayed in your marriage for Him
You gave Him glory
And He promised He would take care of you in return
But He broke His promise

I haven't forgiven Him for that
I can only hope that all that sacrifice you made
And all that *faith* you had in Him wasn't in vain

Karma

I met someone the other day
We exchanged a few texts
Everything was going so well
Until I got blocked
I deserved it, I guess
It was my karma for blocking my ex

"How old are you?" they asked
*"Before I answer your question about my age
What do you think about older women. LOL,"* I replied
What the hell was I thinking?
Why didn't I just answer the question?
But now, they will never know
That I am only four years older than them

My ex was one year older than me
They didn't care about my age
They wanted me
If I had stayed,
I would never have to worry about being too old for anybody

How many have you had?
I've had one before
Have you had a serious relationship before?
It was pretty serious
But it didn't last long because they were abusive
I'm glad I got out of that situation

Why am I such an idiot?
I could've hit send after writing
It was pretty serious

But I had to give unnecessary information
To someone I just met

I received no reply
I understood
Who wants to be with a broken person?
Who would want to deal with all of that baggage?
It's probably my karma for blocking my ex

You can never say I mistreated you
I never put my hands on you
My ex told me
And they were right
Maybe *I* overreacted sometimes
Everybody gets a little angry
We all lose our tempers
We all say things we don't mean
I didn't have to get scared that they would hurt me
Eventually

I could've had more patience
More understanding of what they were going through

My ex begged me to stay
They promised to stop screaming at me, cussing me out,
And calling me names
I promised I would try my best not to piss them off so much
But I didn't keep my promise
I left them
Then I moved

I blocked them, unfollowed them, and deleted their number
Over a year later, no one wants me
Now *I* have to deal with *my* karma

Nothing

When people want me to speak
Though I have plenty on my mind
I stay *quiet*,
I shake my head from left to right
Because I'm too afraid of what they will
Think of me
When I say nothing
They think I have nothing to say

I think about my life a lot
I think about my future
My plans and how
What I want my legacy to be
But I am slow to *act*
So, people think that
I'm doing nothing with my life
And I think that I am nothing

What is my purpose?
What was I placed on this earth?
To accomplish?
It can't be anything,

All the pain and hard lessons
I've had to learn in my short years
So far,
Can't all be for nothing?

Yet at any moment
It can all end, and the only thing
I'll be remembered for

By those, I left behind is
Nothing.

Maybe, I am lying
Maybe they'll remember my smile
The times that I said nothing
Instead of saying something hurtful
The times I said nothing, but I *listened* to
Every word that came out of them because
They were in agony and needed someone to hear their cries

Or maybe they'll remember that
Time is nothing without a purpose
Because I showed them that
I lived my truth, and I walked
On hard grounds
Until I found the perfect shoes
To fit my feet
So that my toes could stop splinting
 and bleed no more
Because I walked
Searching for my purpose

It can't all be for *nothing.*

A Different Kind of Love

This is the year I learn
This is the year I do
Do those things I've never done before
I always thought
Love came from others
So, it made sense that I never
Truly felt it
Until I learned that the greatest love for me
Can only come from within
So, this is the year
I pledge to *do* things differently

Used to Be

I used to be beautiful
I used to be thin
I used to get dates
I used to get compliments
I used to have dreams
I used to think I had time
Now I see that I'm getting old
And there is a good chance
That I'll be spending the rest of my days
In this cold world all alone
Good thing I'm not alone
But I don't think that's something
I'm *supposed* to feel good about

My Beauty Is Not Skin Deep

My beauty is not skin deep
My beauty does not stop with my Brown skin
And my curly hair

My beauty OOZES into my Haitian accent
It sneaks into my quiet nature
So that it can amplify my lauding voice
My beauty is not just my full lips
It's in the words that I speak when I'm
Cheering for my sisters and brothers
My beauty is in the tears that I cry
For the men, women, and children in Syria
Who are caught in a war that makes no sense

My beauty exists in my anger
It exists in the way that I feel frustrated
About a world I cannot change
But I still feel hope in a child's smile
My beauty still believes in love
Forgiveness and compassion

After all I've seen and been through
That should make me believe otherwise
My beauty may not be physical in your eyes
But my beauty is there
And it will still be here
When *every* king has turned to dust

Therapy

Before I even met her
I didn't want to like her

I already had a therapist
Who knew just what to say

Why did I have to stop seeing her
Only to start seeing a new one?

Will I ever *not* need therapy?
I ask myself
If it's helping me
The answer *should* be yes

My new therapist
She makes me take deep breaths
She makes me move
She makes me place my hands on different parts of my body

When I tell her how I feel
She asks me where do I feel it
The hurt, the joy, the pain
She makes me point
To which part of my body it's manifesting

She says that I should be grounded
And get into a place ready to receive
Before we get started

She reads poems to me
She asks me to read poems
Sometimes I do

She makes me tell her things
Things I had never told anyone before
Not even my other therapist

I want to not *feel* shame
I want to *feel* acceptance
I want to *feel* safe

I don't know how many years of therapy
It's going to take

I know that I don't have enough time for this
I don't have time to waste
I don't have time to *not* try

I will keep trying

And do as my therapist told me
Take a deep breath
Ground myself
And be *open* to receive

Safe: A Letter to My Fear

I am safe
I am safe
I am safe

I stand my ground
I stand my ground
I stand my ground

You do *not* control me
You tiny little thing
I can squash you with my pinky toe alone

You have never protected me
Because you're weak
But I am strong

You are nothing
You coward

I am safe now
I am safe
I am *safe*

So This Is Love

Never tell a man you don't like him
Never talk to a man too loudly
I heard these words coming from my home
I don't blame my grandmother
For wanting to teach me how to live

In a world where
Those who are *supposed* to protect me
Are the same ones who see me as their prey
Haitian women giving other Haitian women advice
Or should I say "warnings"
About how to stay *alive*
In a world that is too fragile

Don't be too mean
Never criticize a man
Never disrespect a man
Never ignore a man
And my personal favorite
Don't say no
Because if you do
He might think
You're joking
And he might ask again
Giving you another chance
To correct your mistake
And if you don't make it right by him
Well, whatever you get
Is what you asked for
And then we wonder
Why we live in a world

Where some of us
Are broken
And most of us laugh
When we hear the L-word
Yet
We are women
Yet
We are human
So fragile and so strong

Resilience

I keep surprising myself over and over and over
When I go to sleep at night with thoughts of nothingness
The feeling I should just give up
But then, I wake up in the morning
Ready to battle for another day

I remember the unhappiness of my childhood
But I manage to put it all in the back of my mind
And *live* to smile for another day

Resistance

I refuse to accept that because
I was born into circumstances I had *no* control over
That I have no choice in how *my* life is to be lived

I do not accept when I hear
The words Haitian woman, immigrant, black, shy, quiet
As a way to denigrate *me*

Community

Haitian is not an easy cross to bear
But when I go back home
And when I remember the way things
Are back home
And how life can be beautiful back home
And how it is the only place on this earth
Where I can say with confidence
That I truly belong
I feel safe
I am saved
I belong
I have a place on this earth
A place that *no* one else can fill but me

Protest

I protest every day
No, I do not go out in a crowd
And break windows
Or burn down buildings
Though these actions are justified
When it's done by people who are tired of
Not being *heard*
Being treated like they *don't* matter

I did not go marching after George Floyd's murder
Because I did not want to be the next victim

I protest by existing
I protest by protecting my peace of mind
I protest by staying in my lane
I protest by minding my business
I protest by staying safe inside my house
Cozy under my sheets
In my warm bed

Oh, wait...never mind
I *forgot* Breana Taylor

One Life Taken

One life taken
One life *stolen*
One life shortened
One life not given a chance to see what it could become
One life not given a chance to rest in the fruits of its labor

Many lives destroyed
Many lives *shaken*
Many lives lost
Many lives will never be whole again
Many lives are taken for granted
Many lives paralyzed

One life refuses to move forward
One life too *scared* to see its potential
One life still in the past
One's life peaceful presence is obsolete
One life all alone
Trying to figure out what is its purpose on this earth
One life who knows what its purpose is
But isn't strong enough to see to it that it's fulfilled

One life was taken
One life was *destroyed*
One life was shortened
One life was stolen
One life had to start all over
One life now must *remember* that day forever

Healing

I still don't know how to feel
About this healing thing
This forgiveness thing

I hope I am doing it right
I put things on the back burner

I do not know if I will ever figure it out

Maybe it's by writing my thoughts and feelings down
That I heal
But more trauma keeps coming

And then I write about them some more

Then the next one comes
Maybe that's healing
Maybe that's a *good* thing

Quiet

When you're quiet
You don't get any respect

When you're quiet
They tell you who you are
Instead of asking you

When you're quiet
You're aware that
You must change
Because something is *wrong*
With you

When you're quiet
They assume that
You don't have anything to say

When you're quiet
They are surprised to find
That you can dance
And make them *laugh*

They don't believe it's you
 When they hear
 How loud you can scream

Their shook faces
And raised eyebrows to make you revert to your quiet side
And go back inside your shell

So you learn early

That when they have made up their opinions of
Who you are
They don't like it when you show them different

So, you *keep* your dancing
Between the four walls of your small room
Where there's not even enough space to move the way you want to

You keep silly jokes
To yourself
Because you won't always feel like being funny
You're a black woman
So, people expected you to be the opposite of shy and quiet
When they find out that you're not
They *secretly* think you're faking it

At some point in your life
You muster up enough courage to let a few people
But they must work hard for it
You can't give your trust to just anybody

A pretty journal and a pen
Becomes your best friend
Then when you get a laptop
It becomes like a second mother to you
You tell it everything

Because when you're quiet,
They *assume* that you don't have anything to say

New Beginnings

A new season is coming
I don't know how to feel about it
I wish I could be certain of what is to come

How many times do I have to see
A new beginning?
So many things are changing
So many things are coming to an end

Who will hold my hands?
Will I be left all on my own?
With no one to guide me
No one to correct me when
I don't know what decision to make

A new birthday is coming
A new career
Moving to a new place
No more schooling
No more mentors
No more therapy
Only a shiny diploma
Collecting dust on my wall
And only my pen and paper
And my medications
Will be left with me

The new days coming might be brighter than
The new beginnings I've had to endure in the past
Maybe I'll get the break that
I desperately need and want

I wish I could be certain
Of what will come next
But like I've done in the past
Whatever is to come
I will let it *be*

Later

For all the mountains that I've climbed
I still have a thousand more to go
And I can't help but think
How many more I could've climbed
If not for my *own* cowardice

All the excuses I give myself
To think I thought I was doing myself some good
But deep down, I knew that time would not forgive me

All the wishes I made
You would think I have a fairy godmother
Waiting to make all my desires come true

All the fantasies I have
I have to remind myself that I don't
Live in a dreamland

I try to remember that
Every time I tell myself
Later

Lifetime

I will not look back and think of all the things I could have done
I will not think back and wish for all the things I didn't have

In my next lifetime
I will not want to turn back time to undo what I've done to myself

In my next lifetime
I will not think of my life and ask
What happened or how did I get here

In my next lifetime
I will not wonder
What have I done with this gift I've been giving
What do I have to show for it?
Not much

In my next lifetime
I will not hate any part of me
I will not have ugly memories to keep me up at night

In my next lifetime
I will be protected
And I will be a protector

In my next lifetime
There will be no depression
Or anxiety to get in my way

In my next lifetime
I will be a *force*

I will be a brave soul
I will have a strong spirit

In my next lifetime
My wills will be stronger than my fears

I may not be able to do it all here
But in my next lifetime
I'm going to take over the world

Breakthrough

You no longer control me
You are *nothing* to me
You are less than a speck of dirt underneath my shoes

I no longer believe you
I no longer want you
You are *nothing*

I will not give you to someone else
Because you are destroyed
There is *nothing* to exist
Not in my lifetime
Not in the next one-thousand lifetimes

I am free
If I fall, it is by my fault
Nothing is yours
If I win, it is because I earned it
If make a mistake
It's because I'm human

If everything I do fails
It's because I did not work hard enough
Everything I do
Is of my choosing
Nothing to do with you

I rebuke you
I reject you
I undo you

I forgive you

I break you
Generational curse
From now on
I am free of you
I *am* in control

Holy Motherfuckers

They're everywhere
They're watching you
When they come up to you
They ask you who you are
Bible in hand
They're ready to convert you

They will kill you with politeness
Their smiles are contagious
Before they knew you
They already loved you

They tell you about God's plan for you
They tell you how Jesus died for you
The passion in their voices is enough to kill you

They want your soul
They want your body
They want your blood

And so, you join them in bliss
You raise your hands with them
In unison, you sing their songs

You believe in their prophecies
They tell you about your life
You devote yourself to making
Their prognosis come true

And when you cannot satisfy their every need
They tell you there is a spirit inside you
And they must cast it out

When they finally kill you
You try to run away
But here they go again
Watching you
Smiling at you
Ready to kill you
With their *kindness*

Quiet 2

Why are you so quiet?
That's the question
I get asked by people
Who don't understand
The *power* in my silence

They don't really want an answer
They just want me to know
That *they* know
That something is wrong with me
To know that I'm not like them
That I'm *different*

But am I really different from everybody else?
Because when someone gets close enough to me
I am really warm
I tell them stories
I make them *laugh*
And I leave them wanting *more*

Maybe I am different from everybody else
I wish I had a good answer to their question
But the *last* thing I want is to be alienated even more

Everything Is Going to Be Okay

Things may not be okay right now
Everything may not be going right
Life is meant to be stressful

Without challenges
We wouldn't be anything

The beautiful thing is
Everything is going to be okay
It may not feel like it right now
But later
Everything will turn out okay

You will be okay
I will be okay

As long as we *keep* going

A Good Cry

I cried last night
I don't know why
The tears just came and came
I did not resist them
They poured like a pure stream by a quiet river

I cried last night
There was not one reason why
I just needed to cry
It's been a *long* time since I've had a good cry

Dream

I dreamt
That I *finally* found myself
I am a new person
I no longer *feel* shame
Or the need to apologize
For
Being born

Or for how *I* came to be
Into this world

I know that I *belong*.
I know where I'm going.

I know what I'm doing.
I know what *I'm* doing.
I know what I'm doing.

Breathe

Breathe

Keep breathing

Take another deep breath

And another one

And another one

Now lift your head

Look at your reflection in the mirror

And say

You're going to be okay, girl

Then close your eyes

And *take* another *deep* breath.

Let Go

Let go of the tension in your neck
Let go of the stiffness between your thighs
Let go of the weight in your arms
Let go of the chains on your feet
Let go of the slump on your shoulders
Let go of the dead weight in your heart
Let go of the rocks on your back
Let *go* of the pain in your past

I Hate Writing

I hate writing
With a *passion*
It makes me depressed when I do it
And when I don't do it
I get anxiety that I would never *wish* on
Another human being

My writing is so bad
I don't need to pretend
Maybe one day I'll be
Good *enough*

Would it have been worth it
If writing was easy?
To write about *anything*
To just write

Or did the universe design writing to be that way
So that the stories I write
Are only the ones that are *supposed* to make it on a page

I have a lot of writing inside of me
It is on my mind twenty-four hours a day
Still, I fear most of it will go *with* me to my grave

I wasted too much time
Time that was *precious*
Time that I didn't have

When will it end?
When will I *find* the answer?
The key to write
What I want
When I want
Where I want
And how I want

Writing is a pain in my ass
It stops me from *enjoying* my life
It keeps me from doing other things that I want to do

I do not enjoy it
Most of the time
Until I am *finished*

Then I remember that I have to do it all over again
And I must rewrite it five million *times*
Before it's no longer a pile of dog shit

And that's *why* I hate writing

I Did It Anyway

I didn't feel like writing today
But I did it anyway

I didn't feel like reading today
But I did it anyway

I didn't feel like getting out of bed today
But I did it anyway

I didn't feel like going outside today
But I did it anyway

I didn't feel like brushing my hair today
But I did it anyway

I didn't feel like cleaning the dog poop
I stepped in when I took a walk today
But I did it anyway

I didn't feel like looking at the pictures of my mom
That I hung on my walls today
But I did it anyway

I didn't feel like smiling today
But I *did* it anyway

What If It's True

What if it's true
One day we'll be together again
We'll sit on a rocking chair
Facing a warm sunset
And we'll smile when
We tell each other the stories of our lives

We'll look into each other's eyes
And we'll cry
And we'll laugh
And we'll remember
And we'll forget

What if it's true
All pain and suffering ends
When you close your eyes
For the final time
And only rest and serenity await you

What if it's true
When I talk to you
You hear me
And that you watch me at night when I sleep
To make sure I'm safe
And you walk with me when I'm alone
How much less lonely I would be

What if it's true that when I smile
You smile, too
And when I cry
You share in my pain

And whisper in my ear
That *everything* is going to be okay

Honey

They say honey is a medicine
It can heal the wound that's on your skin
But who will heal the wound that's deep within?

A spoonful of honey with a squeeze of lemon
It will make your throat feel smooth again
But what can soothe the lumps
That are hard as rocks that form inside your throat?
That block your vocal cords when you try to speak your mind

Put some honey on your face
It will erase all of the flaws you think are there
But don't forget about
The tears that will not let your face stay dry

Love is what you're looking for
Because love can be much sweeter than honey
But don't forget
You have to go through the bees to get to the honey
And if you love the flower
You have to love its thorns

But it's still worth it
When you get that honey
The worst that could happen
Is you falling into a coma
Because you've got too much sugar
Running *through* your bloodstream

Killed by Kindness

I am way too nice
I took a white baby to the park
A white grandmother asked me questions
I answered them all
"His parents, they do know you, right?"
She questioned me with a frown on her face
I could have asked her did she ask that question to
Every babysitter she met
Or better yet, I should have told her to fuck off
But I just smiled and said, *"Of course."*

My niceness goes too far sometimes

I sat on my porch
Reading a lovely book
A white couple walked by
The lady asked me, *"Do you own this house?"*
I could have told her that's none of her business
Better yet, I should have asked her who the hell was she
But I smiled and said, "No, I have a landlord."

I am too nice for my own good

A friend of mine unfollowed me
When she posted her stories, I sent her heart emojis
When she posted pictures, I told her that she looked beautiful
Maybe she thought I meant something else
When I just wanted to pay her a compliment

I wonder when will I stop being too nice

About the Author

Judith is a seasoned writer and educator with a background as an ancillary teacher for the Chicago Public School System. She holds a master's in creative writing from Roosevelt University, with a bachelor's in journalism. At the young age of 11 years old, Judith started her journey from Haiti to America.

Judith has endured her fair share of life's ups & downs. As a "diaspora," she has come a long way. She has two long-form manuscripts in the works and a laundry list of goals. We can say she is just getting started.

Judith currently works as a book coach, editor, blogger, and designer in Chicago, Illinois.

Connect with Judith:

www.judithanniquefrancois.com
Instagram: @judithanniquefrancois
Twitter: @AnniqueFrancois
Email: workwithme@judithanniquefrancois.com

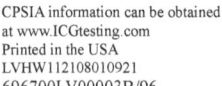

CPSIA information can be obtained
at www.ICGtesting.com
Printed in the USA
LVHW112108010921
696700LV00003B/96